NOËL!

CAROLS AND ANTHEMS
FOR ADVENT, CHRISTMAS & EPIPHANY
FOR MIXED VOICE CHOIRS

Selected & edited by David Hill

THE NOVELLO CHORAL PROGRAMME

FRONT COVER *Nativity* (c.1913-14, painted limestone) by Eric Gill (1882-1940)
by kind permission of The Eric Gill Estate and the Bridgeman Art Library
BACK COVER photograph of David Hill by John Crook

COVER DESIGN Susan Clarke

MUSIC SETTING Stave Origination

ISBN 0-7119-8455-7

© Copyright 2000 Novello & Company Ltd.
Published in Great Britain by Novello Publishing Limited.

HEAD OFFICE
14/15 Berners Street,
 London W1T 3LJ
UK
Tel. +44 (0)20 7612 7400
Fax +44 (0)20 7612 7546

SALES AND HIRE
Music Sales Distribution Centre,
Newmarket Road,
Bury St. Edmunds,
Suffolk IP33 3YB
UK
Tel +44 (0)1284 702600
Fax +44 (0)1284 768301

www.musicsales.com
e-mail: music@musicsales.co.uk

Contents

Introduction

The forty-seven carols and anthems in *Noël!* have been chosen to serve the needs of all types of Christmas choral occasions. The content is wide ranging, so that the selection in the book will be useful to choirs of differing sizes and standards. At the core of this musical anthology are those best known and seemingly timeless carols which should appear in any collection which claims to be comprehensive. Additionally, there are many new arrangements (including *Away in a manger, Jingle bells, It came upon the midnight clear, Once in royal David's city, Rocking*), and works by contemporary composers Richard Rodney Bennett, Judith Bingham, John Tavener and Judith Weir to provide the adventurous with new challenges.

The repertoire for choirs is broadening all the time and *Noël!* is a reflection of modern trends in choral music: increasing diversity of style and period whilst remaining accessible to today's groups of amateur singers.

I should like to thank my colleagues at Novello for their advice and expertise; in particular Liz Robinson, Olivia Kilmartin and Howard Friend and the Novello Choral Advisors, Ralph Allwood, Brian Kay and Barry Rose.

David Hill
Winchester, June 2000

The angel Gabriel from heaven came

Sabine Baring-Gould

Basque trad., arr. Edgar Pettman

3. Then gentle Mary meekly bowed her head;
   'To me be as it pleaseth God!' she said.
   'My soul shall laud and magnify his holy Name.'
   Most highly favoured lady! Gloria!

4. Of her Emmanuel, the Christ, was born,
   In Bethlehem, all on a Christmas morn;
   And Christian folk throughout the world will ever say:
   Most highly favoured lady! Gloria!

Adam lay ybounden

15th century

Boris Ord

3. Ne had the ap-ple tak-en been, The ap-ple tak-en been,___

Ne had nev-er our___ la - dy A - been hea-ven-é___ queen.

4. Bless - ed be the time___ That ap - ple tak-en was,

There - fore we moun sing - en, De-o gra - ci - as, De-o
gra - - - - ci - as, De - o gra - - - ci - as!
gra - ci - as,___ De - o gra - ci - as!
- as, De - o gra - - - - ci - as!

To Alice and Susannah

Away in a manger

William J. Kirkpatrick
arr. David Hill

e - ver, and watch me, I pray; Bless all the dear children in thy tender care, And fit us for heaven to live with thee there.

(ah) ah

(ah) ah

Balulalow

James, John and Robert Wedderburn

Peter Warlock

hert And ne - ver mair from thee de -

-pert. But

S. Mm———— Mm——

A. Mm———————— Ah——

T. Mm———————— Ah——

B. Mm———— Ah——

poco rit.

a tempo

Chorus alone

Chorus

(+16')

Bethlehem Down

Bruce Blunt

Peter Warlock

grave - sheets,
dream - ing,

3. When he is King they will clothe_ him in grave - - sheets,_
4. Here he has peace and a short_ while for dream - ing,_

Myrrh for em-balm-ing, and wood for_ a crown,_
Close-hud-dled_ ox-en to keep him_ from cold,_

He_ that lies_ now_ in the_ white_ arms_ of_ Ma - ry,
Ma - ry for_ love, and for_ lul - la - by_ mu - sic

Sleep - ing so_ light - ly_ on Beth - le - hem Down._
Songs_ of a_ shep - herd by Beth - le - hem fold._

dedicated with thanks to Lady Digby

The Clouded Heaven

Lancelot Andrewes and
William Wordsworth

Judith Bingham

* One half sing 'ah', the other half 'uh'
† lower part optional until bar 11 and to a convenient vowel

15

(close on 'n')

Ding dong! merrily on high

G.R. Woodward

16th century French tune
harmonized by Charles Wood

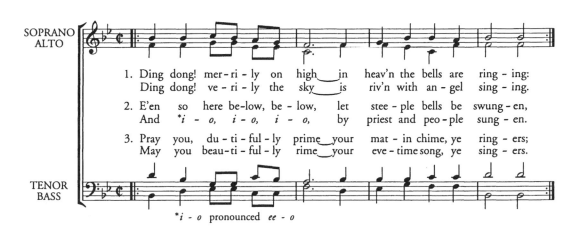

1. Ding dong! mer-ri-ly on high in heav'n the bells are ring-ing:
Ding dong! ve-ri-ly the sky is riv'n with an-gel sing-ing.

2. E'en so here be-low, be-low, let stee-ple bells be swung-en,
And *i - o, i - o, i - o, by priest and peo-ple sung-en.

3. Pray you, du-ti-ful-ly prime your mat - in chime, ye ring-ers;
May you beau-ti-ful-ly rime your eve - time song, ye sing-ers.

*i - o pronounced ee - o

Glo - - - - - - - - - -

- - - - ri - a, Ho - san - na in ex - cel - sis!

Words reprinted from *The Cambridge Carol Book* by permission of SPCK

For David Hill
Commissioned by the Dean and Chapter of Winchester Cathedral
for the enthronement of the new Bishop on January 6th 1996,
sung by the Cathedral Choir, conducted by David Hill

Epiphany

Words and music by Judith Bingham

* One half sing 'ah', the other half hum.

Their star has ri - sen in our hearts,_____ Emp -

Their star has ri - sen in our hearts,_____

our hearts,_____

- ty thrones, a - ban - doned fears,_____

fears,_____

Emp - ty thrones, a - ban - doned fears,_____

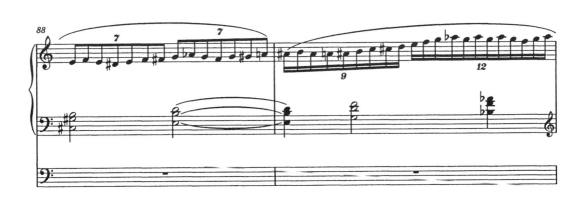

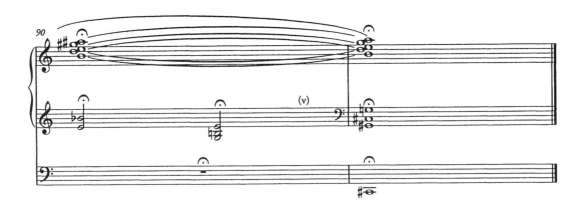

for Martin Neary

God is with us

Text adapted from the Orthodox Great Compline
for Christmas Eve

John Tavener

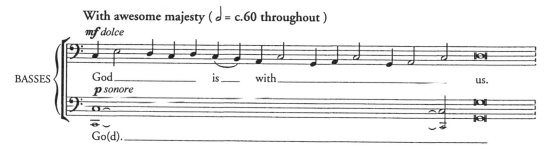

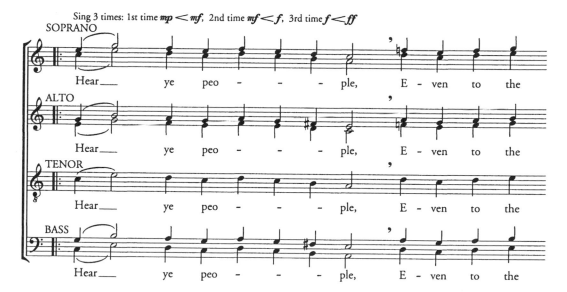

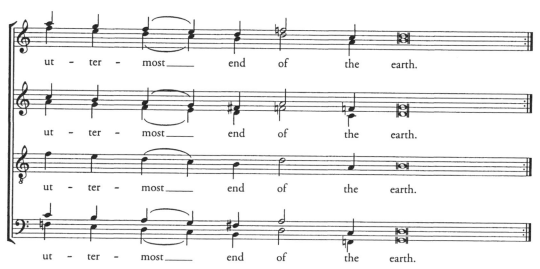

Declaim freely, in Byzantine style

The peo-ple that walked in dark - - - ness have seen a great light. The peo-ple that dwell in the sha - -dow of death, u-pon them the light has shined. For un-to us a child is born! For un-to us a son is given! And

God is with
Go(d).*

God is with
Go(d).*

God is with
Go(d).*

† ♮ denotes a microtone, a characteristic 'break in the voice' of Byzantine chant
* Breathe when necessary, but not simultaneously.
** The soloist should sing from a different point, away from the main body of the choir.

the go - vern-ment shall be u - pon his shoul - der; And_ his

us.

us.

us.

Solo T.

name shall be called Won - - - - - - der - ful! Coun -

40

is ___ born! Christ ___ is born!

is ___ born! Christ ___ is born!

is ___ born! Christ ___ is born!

is ___ born! Christ ___ is born!

is ___ born! Christ ___ is born!

is ___ born! Christ ___ is born!

is ___ born! Christ ___ is born!

Full organ   Sw.   Sw. *molto f*   Full organ

Katounia Limni
13th October 1987

God rest you merry, gentlemen

Trad., arr. David Hill

Verses 1-4 can be sung in unison or in harmony.

3. The shepherds at those tidings
   Rejoicèd much in mind,
   And left their flocks a-feeding,
   In tempest, storm and wind,
   And went to Bethlehem straightway
   This blessèd babe to find:
   O tidings of comfort and joy.

4. But when to Bethlehem they came,
   Whereat this infant lay,
   They found him in a manger,
   Where oxen feed on hay;
   His mother Mary kneeling,
   Unto the Lord did pray:
   O tidings of comfort and joy.

Hark! the herald angels sing

C. Wesley, G. Whitefield,
M. Madan and others

Mendelssohn
Descant and organ part by
David Hill

more may die,___ Born___ to raise the sons of earth

more may die,___ Born to raise the sons of earth

Born to give___ them se - cond birth. *Hark!*___ the he - rald

Born to___ give them se - cond birth. *Hark!* the he - rald

an - gels sing Glo - ry___ to___ the___ new - born King.

an - gels sing Glo - ry___ to the new - born King.

I sing of a maiden

Lennox Berkeley

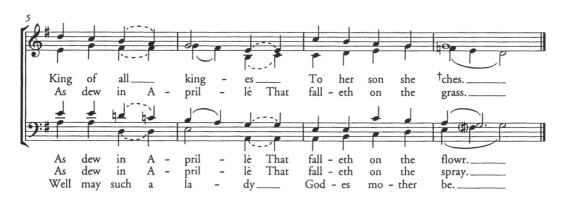

* *makèless* = matchless.
† *ches* = chose.

Illuminare, Jerusalem

15th century
Bannatyne MS *f.*27v

Judith Weir

[1] = star   [2] = king

¹ = at once, all together

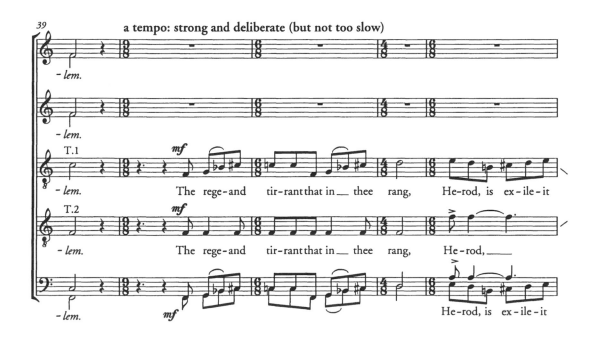

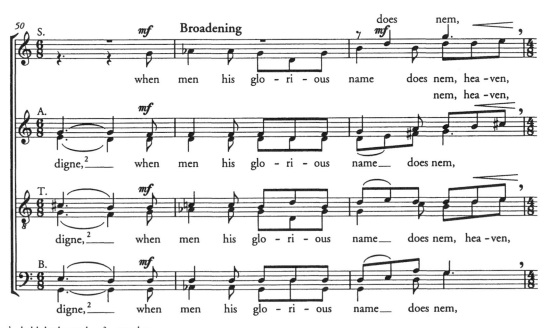

¹ = held, harboured   ² = worthy

In dulci jubilo

arr. J.S. Bach

For a translation, see p.266

© Copyright 2000 Novello & Company Limited

For the Choir of Grimsby Parish Church

In the bleak mid-winter

Christina Rossetti

Robert Walker

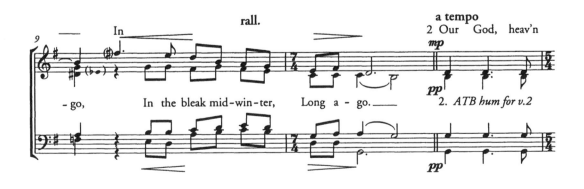

October 1972

It came upon the midnight clear

Edmund H. Sears

Trad., adapted Arthur Sullivan
Descant by David Hill

3. Yet with the woes of sin and strife
   The world has suffered long:
   Beneath the angels' strain have rolled
   Two thousand years of wrong,
   And man, at war with man, hears not
   The love-song which they bring:
   O hush the noise, ye men of strife,
   And hear the angels sing!

4. And ye, beneath life's crushing load,
   Whose forms are bending low,
   Who toil along the climbing way
   With painful steps and slow,
   Look now! for glad and golden hours
   Come swiftly on the wing;
   O rest beside the weary road,
   And hear the angels sing!

o – ver the earth its an – cient splen – dours fling,

all the earth its an – cient splen – dours fling, And

And the whole earth the song the an – gels sing.

the whole world give‿ back the song Which‿ now‿ the an – gels sing.

It came upon the midnight clear

Edmund H. Sears

Richard Storrs Willis
arr. Barry Rose

Jingle bells

J. Pierpont

J. Pierpont,
arr. Ralph Allwood

* 1st tenor may be sung by altos till bar 12

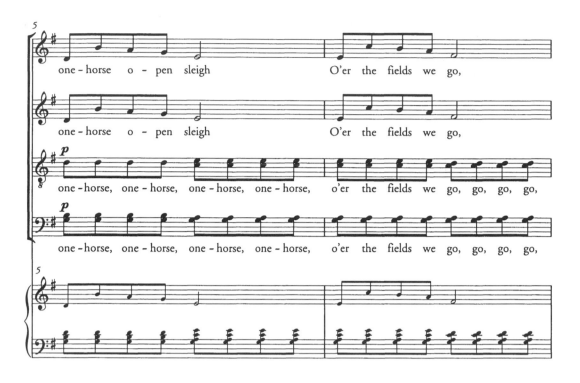

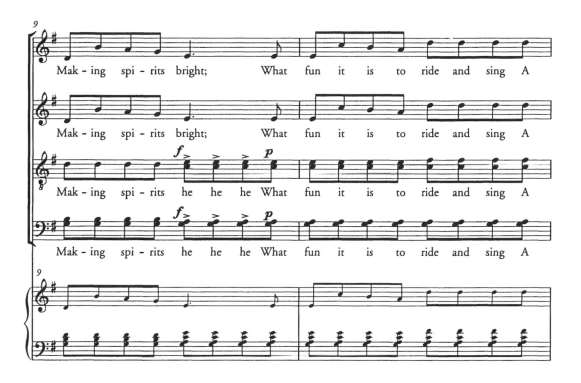

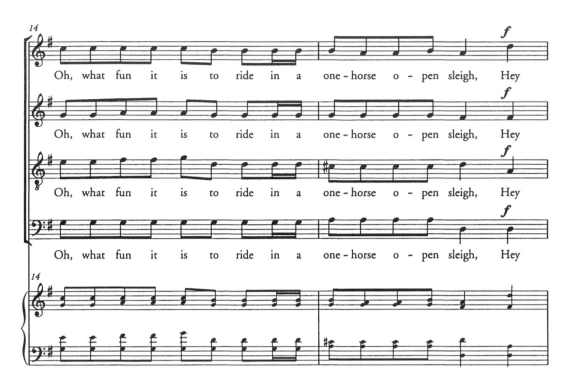

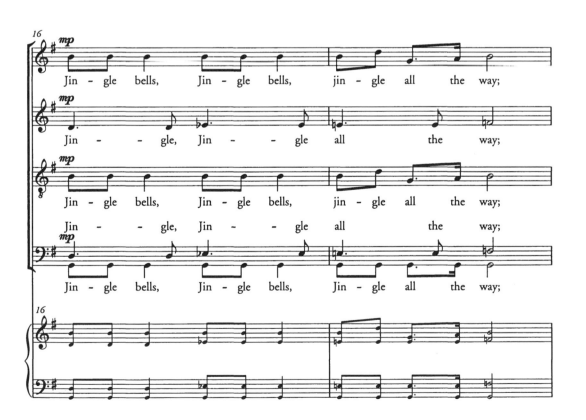

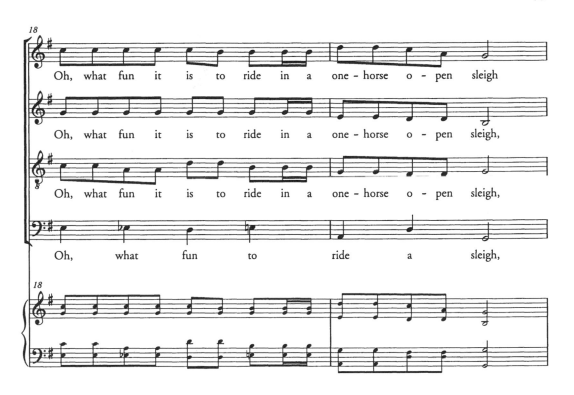

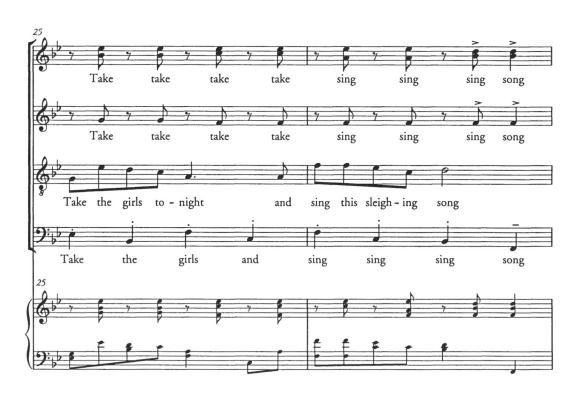

Oh, what fun it is to ride in a one-horse o-pen sleigh

O, what fun it is to ride in a one-horse o-pen sleigh hey! *

* This shout should be short, loud and high in the voice.

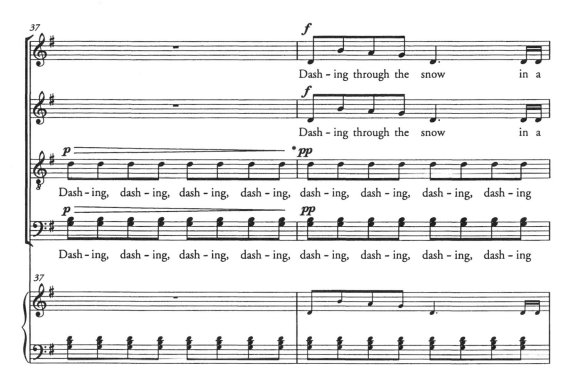

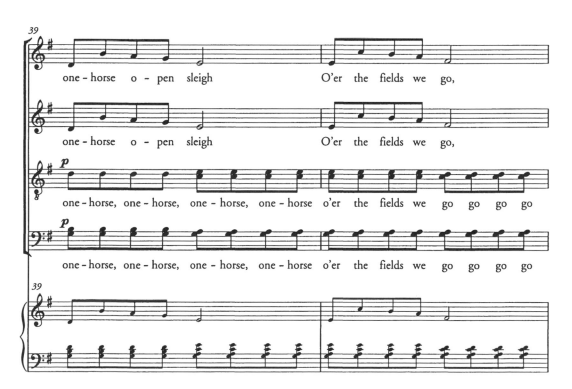

* 1st tenor may be sung by altos till bar 46

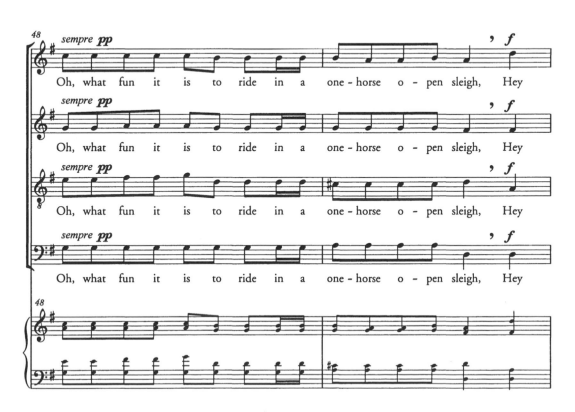

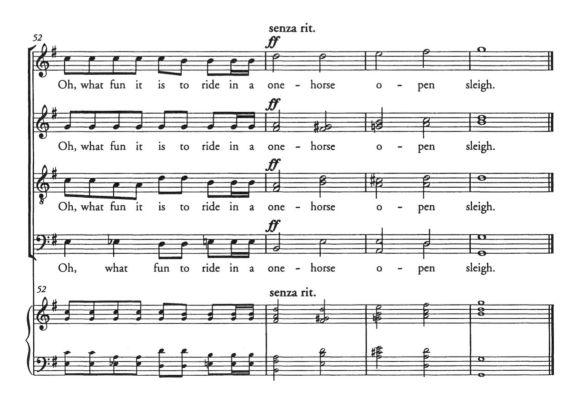

The Kings

(Three kings had journey'd from lands afar)

Translations: solo text by W.G. Rothery,
chorale by William Mercer

Chorale melody by Philipp Nicolai
Solo melody and German text by Peter Cornelius

This work can be performed by
a) solo voice and piano/organ
b) solo voice and choir or
c) solo voice, choir and piano/organ.

English translation of solo text © Copyright 1906 Novello & Company Limited
This arrangement © Copyright 2000 Novello & Company Limited

star___ shin - ing on be - fore, The kings then led to the
-glän - zet des Ster - nes Schein; zum Stal - le ge - hen die

O Right - eous Branch, O
Du Sohn Da - vids aus

low - ly door, They see the Child in a man - ger___ bare, And fall be -
Kön' - ge ein; das Knäb - lein schau - en sie won - nig - lich, an - be - tend

Jes - se's Rod! Thou Son of
Ja - kobs Stamm, mein Kö - nig

shin-ing bright and clear   To those who seek _ it _ doth yet ap - pear;
hal - te treu - lich Schritt!   *Die Kön' - ge wan - dern, _ O wand - re mit!*

- sus, _   Je - - - sus!
- *lich, _*   *freund - - lich, _*

etwas bewegter werdend
Un poco più mosso

The star of mer - cy in peace will bring The pil - grim who seek - eth the heav'n - ly
Der Stern der Lie - be, der Gna - de Stern er - hel - le dein Ziel, so du suchst den

Ho - ly, ho - ly, _ Yet most low - ly, _
schön und herr - lich, _ gross und ehr - lich, _

etwas bewegter werdend
Un poco più mosso

for Simon's 3rd birthday

The Lamb

William Blake

John Tavener

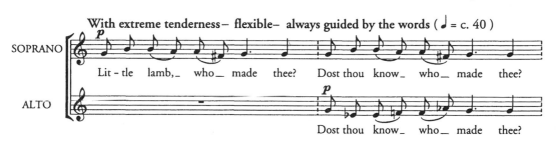

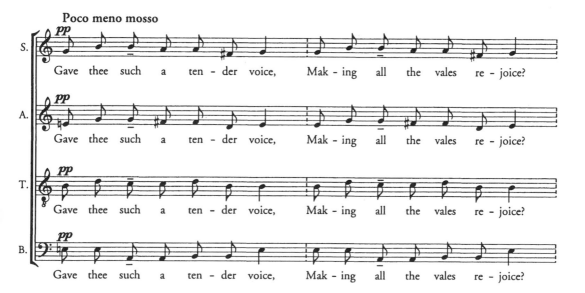

A tempo – moving forward

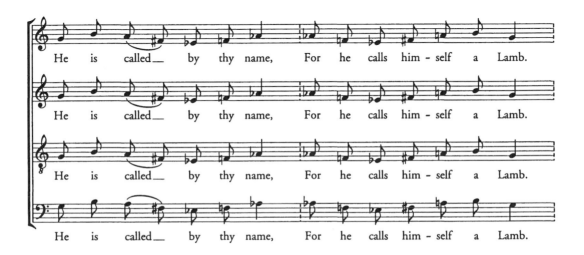

poco

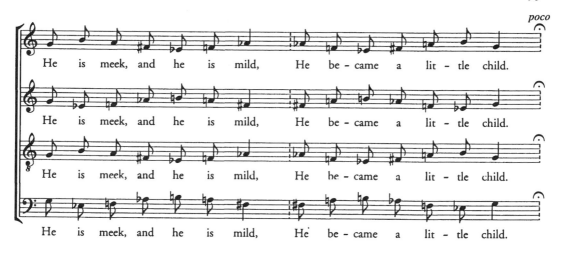

He is meek, and he is mild, He be-came a lit-tle child.

He is meek, and he is mild, He be-came a lit-tle child.

He is meek, and he is mild, He be-came a lit-tle child.

He is meek, and he is mild, He be-came a lit-tle child.

Poco meno mosso

pp

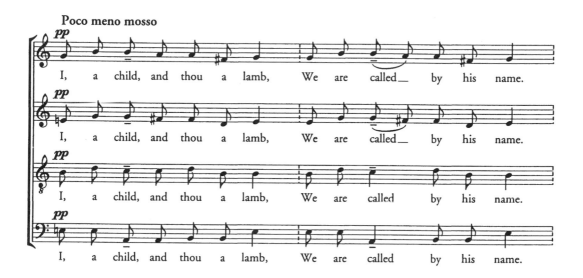

I, a child, and thou a lamb, We are called by his name.

I, a child, and thou a lamb, We are called by his name.

I, a child, and thou a lamb, We are called by his name.

I, a child, and thou a lamb, We are called by his name.

rit.

Lit-tle lamb, God bless thee! Lit-tle lamb, God bless thee!

Lit-tle lamb, God bless thee! Lit-tle lamb, God bless thee!

Lit-tle lamb, God bless thee! Lit-tle lamb, God bless thee!

Lit-tle lamb, God bless thee! Lit-tle lamb, God bless thee!

Long the night

Alick Rowe

Ukrainian melody,
arr. Roy Massey

Lully, lulla, thou little tiny child

The Pageant of the Shearman and Tailors,
Coventry, 15th century

Kenneth Leighton

No small wonder

Paul Wigmore

Paul Edwards

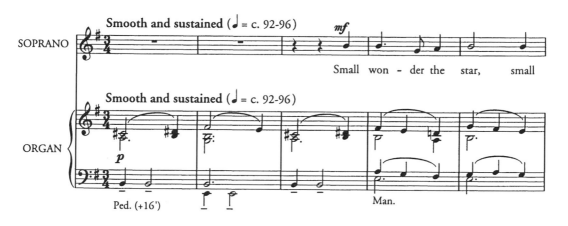

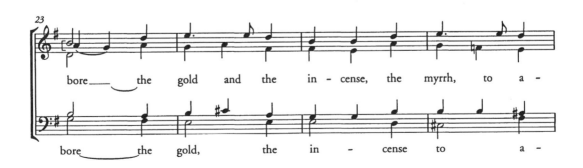

-dore;___ but God gives his life on a cross ___

no___ small___ won - der! Small

won - der the love, small won - der the grace, the

Noël nouvelet

English words by
Marion Jackson

trad. French carol
arr. Stephen Jackson

2. L'an - ge dis - ait: 'Pas - teurs, par - tez d'i - ci,
2. 'Shep-herds from the fields, let glad - ness_ fill your mind.

L'â-me en re - pos et le coeur_ré-jou - i; En Beth-lé - em* trou-
Go to Beth-le - hem, the Lamb of_God to find!' Lo, from the sky the

-ver-ez l'ag - ne - let.' No - ël nou - ve - let, No - ël chant-ons_ i -
an - gel voi - ces sing 'No-el Nou - ve - let' for Christ the_ new-born

* Bett-lé-emm

111

* pronounce 's' in 'tous'

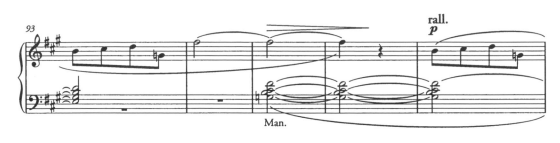

* 'st' not pronounced

O come, all ye faithful
(Adeste, fideles)

Tr. F. Oakeley,
W.T. Brooke
and others

Words and melody by
J.F. Wade (*c.* 1711-1786)
arranged by David Willcocks

1. O come, all ye faith-ful, Joy-ful and tri-um-phant, O
2. God of God, Light of Light,

come ye, O come ye to Beth-le-hem;
Lo! he ab-hors not the Vir-gin's womb;

Come and be-hold him Born the King of An-gels: O
Ve-ry God, Be-got-ten, not cre-a-ted: O

Man.

come, let us a-dore him, O come, let us a-dore him, O

Ped.

come, let us a-dore him, Christ the Lord:

Note: Verses 1-5 may be sung by unison voices and organ, S.A.T.B. voices and organ, or voices unaccompanied as desired.
Verses 3-5 may be omitted. The harmonies used for verses 1-5 are from *The English Hymnal.*

3. See how the shepherds,
   Summoned to his cradle,
Leaving their flocks, draw nigh with lowly fear;
   We too will thither
   Bend our joyful footsteps:
      O come, etc.

4. Lo! star-led chieftains,
   Magi, Christ adoring,
Offer him incense, gold, and myrrh;
   We to the Christ Child
   Bring our hearts' oblations:
      O come, etc.

5. Child, for us sinners
   Poor and in the manger,
Fain we embrace thee, with awe and love;
   Who would not love thee,
   Loving us so dearly?
      O come, etc.

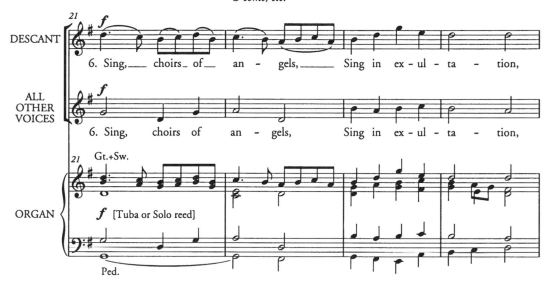

ALL VOICES

O come, all ye faithful

Alternative version of verses 6 and 7

arranged by David Hill

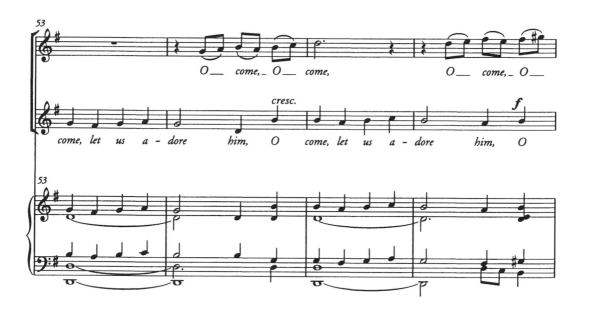

O little town of Bethlehem

Phillips Brooks

Trad., arr. R. Vaughan Williams
Descant by David Hill

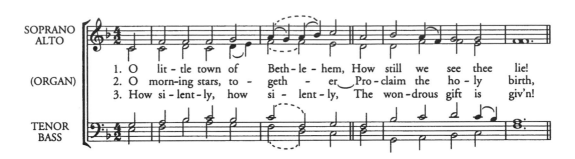

1. O lit - tle town of Beth - le - hem, How still we see thee lie!
2. O morn - ing stars, to - geth - er Pro - claim the ho - ly birth,
3. How si - lent - ly, how si - lent - ly, The won - drous gift is giv'n!

A - bove thy deep and dream - less sleep The si - lent stars go by.
And prais - es sing to God the King, And peace to men on earth;
So God im - parts to hu - man hearts The bless - ings of his heav'n.

Yet in thy dark streets shin - eth The ev - er - last - ing light;
For Christ is born of Ma - ry; And, gath - ered all a - bove,
No ear may hear his com - ing; But in this world of sin,

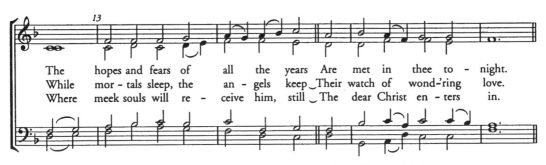

The hopes and fears of all the years Are met in thee to - night.
While mor - tals sleep, the an - gels keep Their watch of wond - 'ring love.
Where meek souls will re - ceive him, still The dear Christ en - ters in.

English traditional melody collected, arranged, and harmonized by Ralph Vaughan Williams (1872-1958)
from *The English Hymnal*, by permission of Oxford University Press.
Verse 4 arrangement and descant by David Hill © 2000 Oxford University Press

O magnum mysterium

Morten Lauridsen

and a sign of great wonder

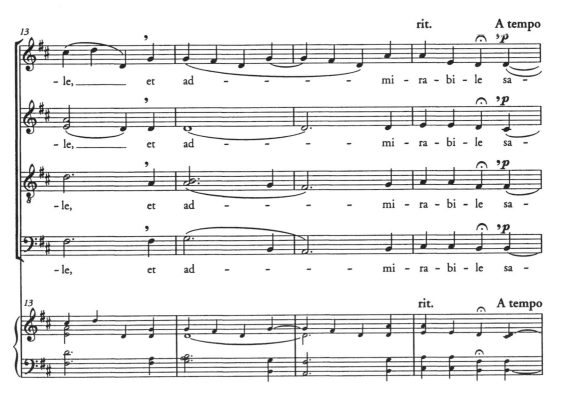

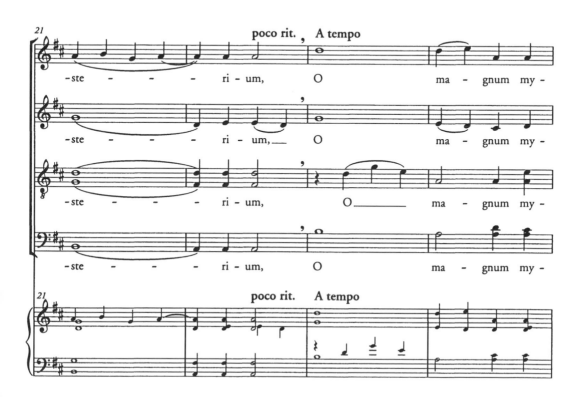

that living creatures should see the Lord

to bear Christ the Lord.

Alleluia!

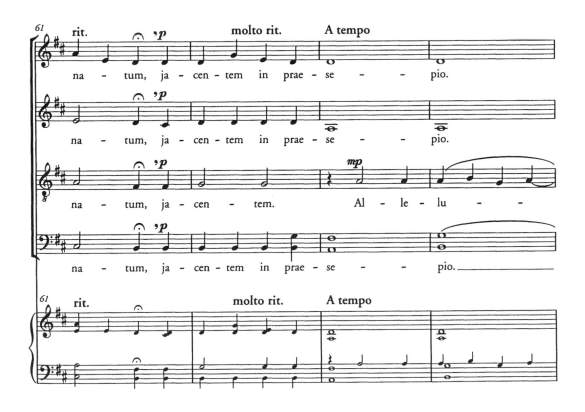

O magnum mysterium

T.L. de Victoria

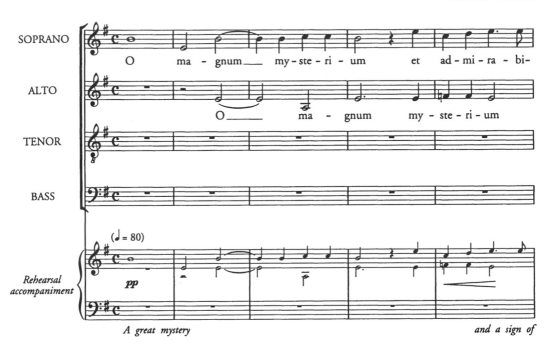

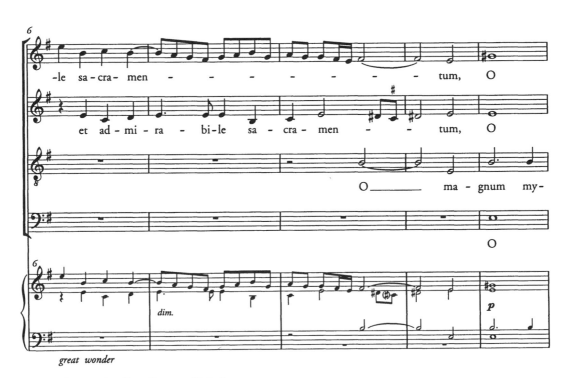

that living creatures

should see the Lord born,

lying in an animal stall!

Blessed

was worthy to bear Christ the Lord.

Of the Father's love begotten

Aurelius C. Prudentius
trans. John Mason Neale

Trad., arr. Richard Lloyd

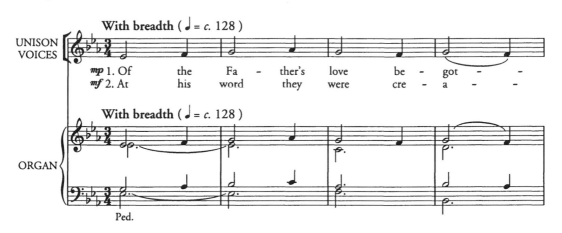

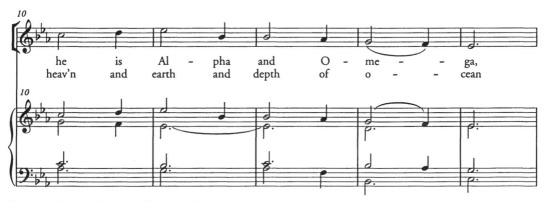

Verse 1 may be sung by men, v.2 by upper voices.

© Copyright 2000 Novello & Company Limited

148

On Christmas day
To my heart

Clement Paman
(c. 1660)

Richard Rodney Bennett

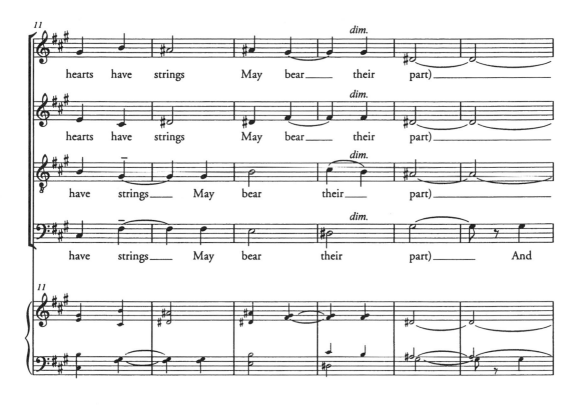

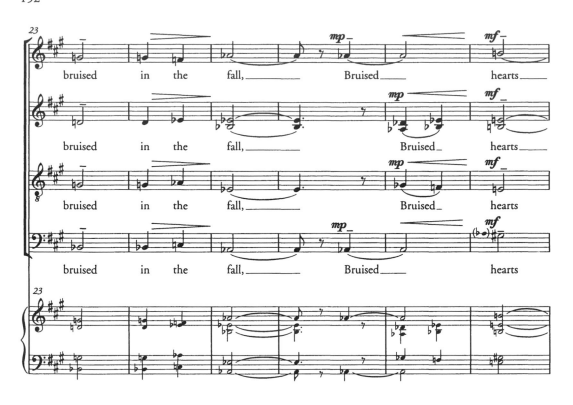

bruised in the fall,_____ Bruised_____ hearts_____

bruised in the fall,_____ Bruised_ hearts_____

bruised in the fall,_____ Bruised_ hearts

bruised in the fall,_____ Bruised_____ hearts

pochiss. rit.

_____ may reach an hum - ble pas - - to - ral.

may reach an hum - ble pas - - to - ral.

may reach_____ a pas - to - ral._____

may reach_____ a pas - to - ral._____

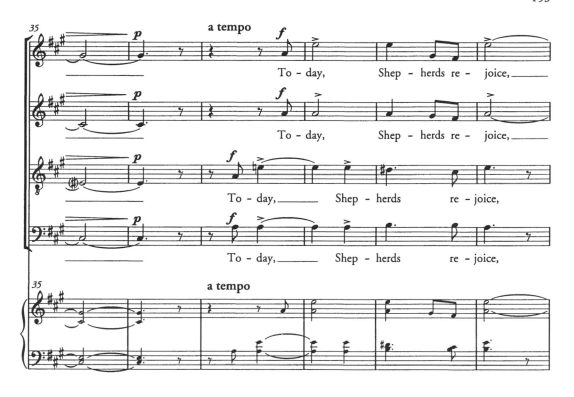

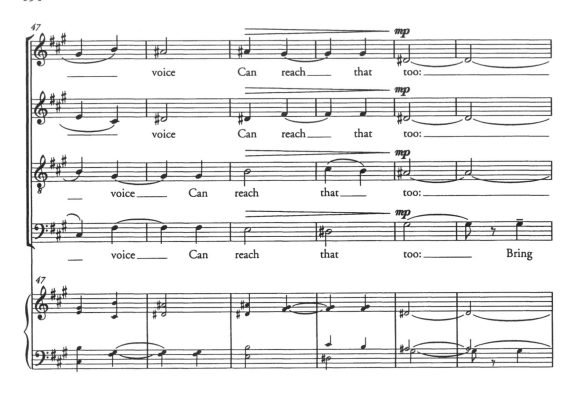

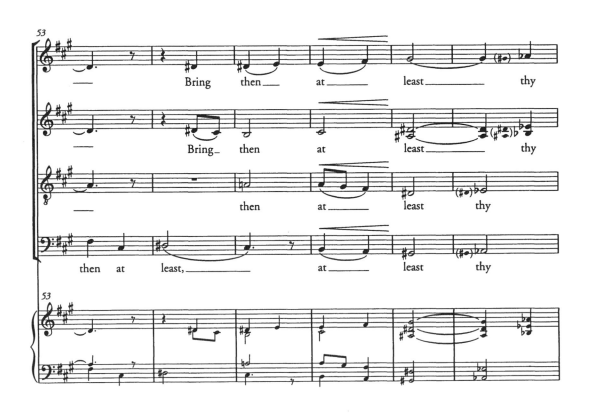

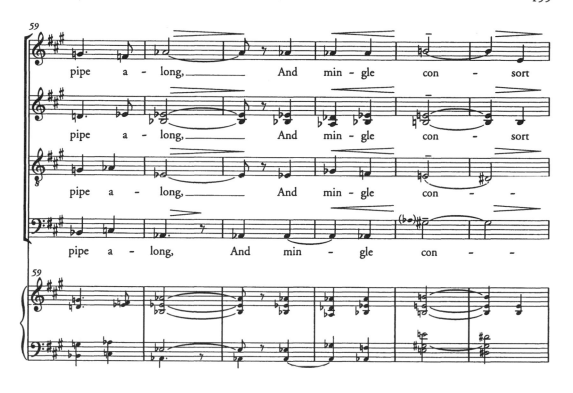

pipe a - long,_____ And min - gle con - sort
pipe a - long,_____ And min - gle con - sort
pipe a - long,_____ And min - gle con - -
pipe a - long, And min - gle con - -

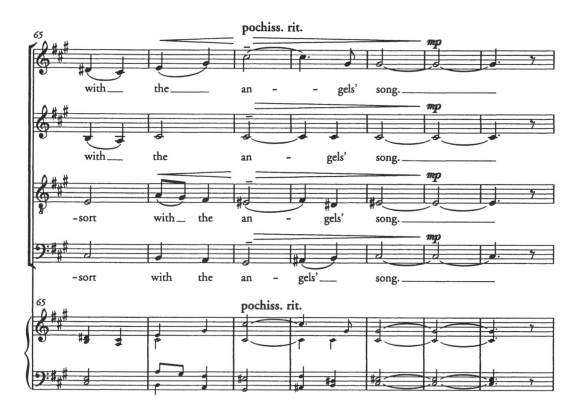

with___ the___ an - - gels' song._____
with___ the an - gels' song._____
-sort with___ the an - gels' song._____
-sort with the an - gels'___ song._____

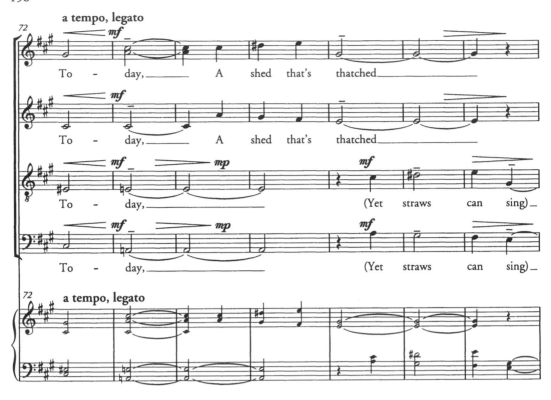

bleat,_____ and ox-en bel-low_____ praise._____

bleat,_____ and ox-en bel-low_____ praise._____

_____ ox — en bel - low_ praise._____

_____ and ox — en bel - low_ praise._____

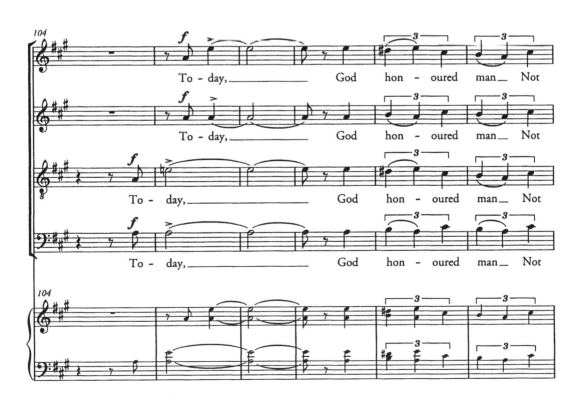

To - day,_____ God hon - oured man_ Not

To - day,_____ God hon - oured man_ Not

To - day,_____ God hon - oured man_ Not

To - day,_____ God hon - oured man_ Not

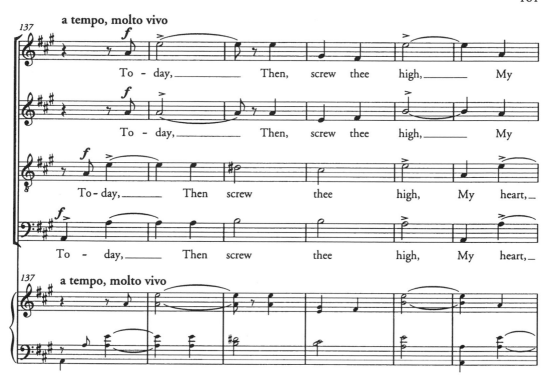

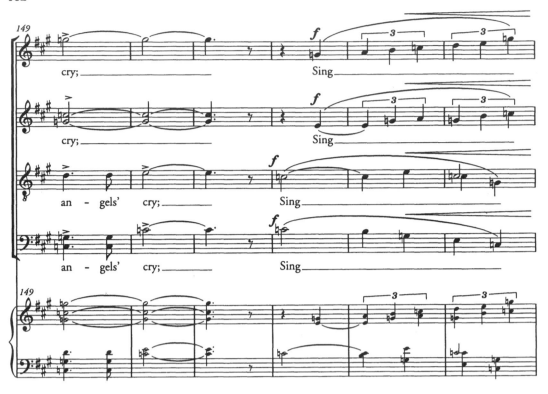

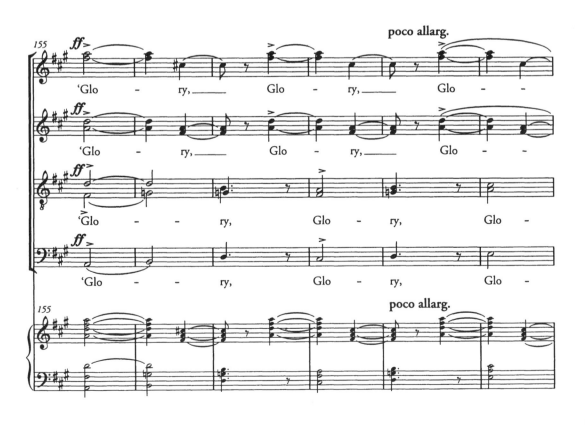

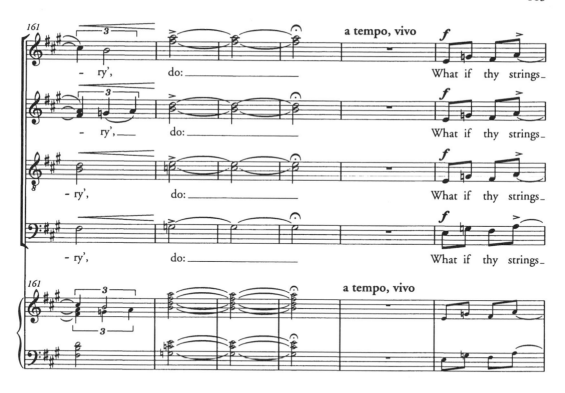

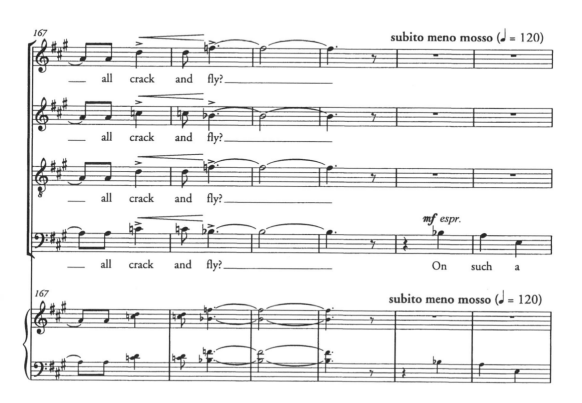

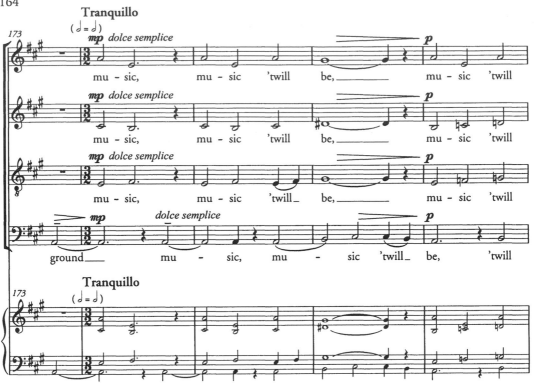

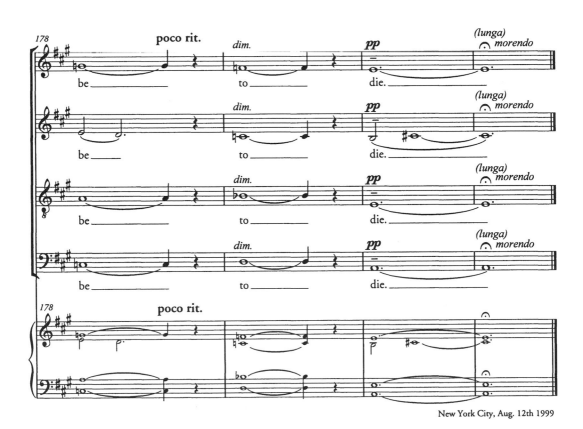

110
ff
mf
an - gels: yet They sing; and can
an - gels: yet They sing; and can
an - gels: yet They sing; and can
an - gels: yet They sing; and can
110
117
Raised man for - get? Praise is our debt to - day,
Raised man for - get? Praise is our debt to - day,
Raised man for - get? Praise is our debt to - day,
Raised man for - get? Praise is our debt to - day,
117

New York City, Aug. 12th 1999

Once in royal David's city

C. F. Alexander

H. J. Gauntlett
harmonized by A. H. Mann
verses 3 & 6 arranged
by James O'Donnell

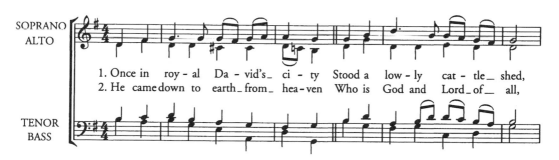

1. Once in roy-al Da-vid's_ ci-ty Stood a low-ly cat-tle_ shed,
2. He came down to earth_ from_ hea-ven Who is God and Lord_ of_ all,

Where a mo-ther laid_ her_ ba-by In a man-ger for_ his_ bed:
And his shel-ter was_ a_ sta-ble, And his cra-dle was_ a_ stall;

Ma-ry_ was that mo-ther mild,_ Je-sus_ Christ_ her lit-tle_ child._
With_ the_ poor and mean and low-ly Lived_ on_ earth_ our Sa-viour ho-ly.

vv. 3&6 overleaf

4. For he is our childhood's pattern,
   Day by day like us he grew,
   He was little, weak, and helpless,
   Tears and smiles like us he knew:
   And he feeleth for our sadness,
   And he shareth in our gladness.

5. And our eyes at last shall see him,
   Through his own redeeming love,
   For that child so dear and gentle
   Is our Lord in heaven above;
   And he leads his children on
   To the place where he is gone.

166

3. And through all his won - drous_child-hood He would hon - our and_ o -

-bey, Love and watch the low - ly_ maid-en, In whose gen - tle arms_he_

lay: Chris-tian chil - dren all must be Mild, o - be - dient, good_as_ he.

* The repeated notes should be slightly articulated

For James Dickie and the Marlborough College Chapel Choir

Out of your sleep

15th century

Robin Nelson

* Corruption of *hele* = spiritual health.

Ped. 16'

174

Marlborough, December 1998

Rocking

Czech carol
arr. David Hill

Arranged from 'Rocking', *Oxford Book of Carols*, 1928, 1964 by permission. Melody collected and edited by Martin Shaw. Czech text 'Hajej, nynjej, transferred by Percy Dearmer.

176

* cue-sized notes are for rehearsal only

Ped. to Man., 16'

Ped. 16'

See, amid the winter's snow

Edward Caswall

John Goss,
arr. Richard Lloyd

TENORS & BASSES

1. See, a - mid the win - ter's snow, Born for us on earth be - low,
4. 'As we watched at dead of night, Lo! we saw a won - drous light;

ORGAN

Man.

See, the ten - der Lamb ap - pears, Pro - mised from e - ter - nal years!
An - gels, sing - ing "Peace on earth", Told us of the Sa - viour's birth.'

REFRAIN: full harmony, with organ

S.
A.

Hail, thou e - ver - bless - ed morn! Hail, Re - demp - tion's hap - py __ dawn!

T.
B.

Sing through all Je - ru - sa - lem: __ 'Christ is born in Beth - le - hem!'

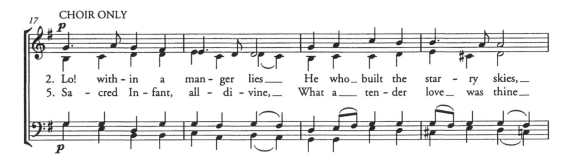

CHOIR ONLY

2. Lo! with-in a man-ger lies__ He who__ built the star-ry skies,__
5. Sa - cred In-fant, all-di-vine,__ What a__ ten-der love__ was thine__

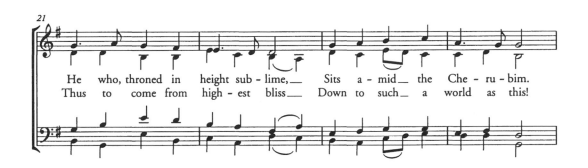

He who, throned in height sub-lime,__ Sits a-mid__ the Che-ru-bim.
Thus to come from high-est bliss__ Down to such__ a world as this!

Hail, thou e-ver-bless-ed morn!__ Hail, Re-demp-tion's hap-py dawn!__

Sing through all Je - ru-sa-lem:__ 'Christ is born__ in Beth-le-hem!'

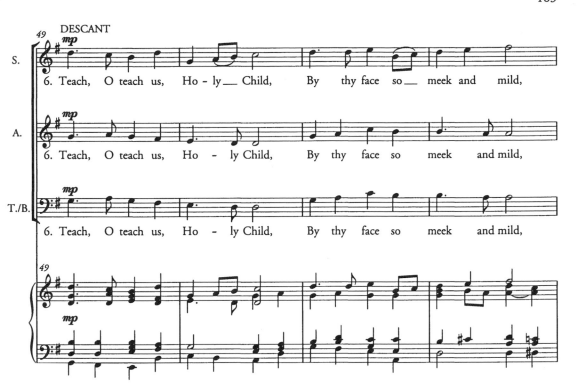

Silent night

Joseph Mohr

Franz Gruber, arr. Barry Rose

So said the angel

Words and music
Peter Skellern

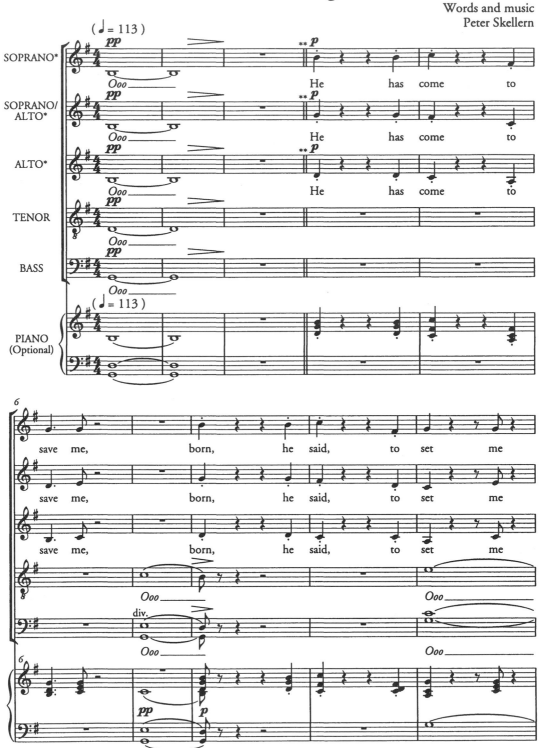

* Women's voices divided into three equal parts
** These staccatos are crisp, but not 'cold'.

No.6 of *Six Simple Carols* (NOV 290698)

* Descant voices taken from Soprano

Still, still, still

trad. German,
translated Andrew Gant

Andrew Gant

still, __ still, __ still, let __ all God's __ world be __ still.

still, _____ still, _____ still, still, _____

still, still, still, still, _____

still, _____

SOPRANOS + BARITONE SOLO

Love, __ love, __ love, my __ heart is __ filled with __ love. The world from __ night is

Love, _____ love, love, __ love,

Love, love, _____ love, __ love,

Love, _____ love, love, _____

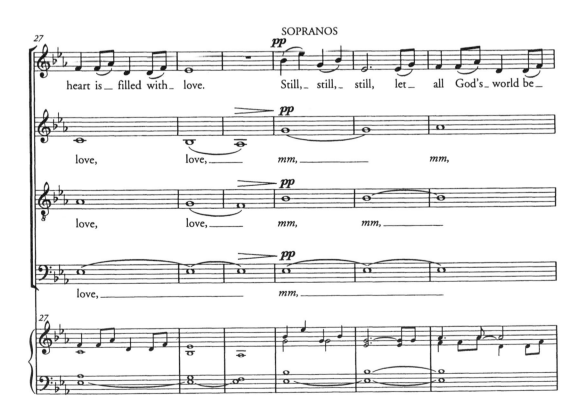

to Karen

Sing lullaby!

Sabine Baring-Gould

Basque trad., arr. David Hill

3. Sing lullaby!
   Lullaby baby, now a-dozing,
   Sing lullaby!
   Hush! do not wake the infant King!
   Soon comes the Cross, the nails, the piercing,
   Then in the grave at last reposing;
   Sing lullaby!

4. Sing lullaby!
   Lullaby, is the Babe a-waking?
   Sing lullaby!
   Hush! do not wake the infant King!
   Dreaming of Easter, gladsome morning,
   Conquering death, its bondage breaking;
   Sing lullaby!

There is no rose

15th century

Arnold Bax, arr. Hubert Dawkes

* cue-sized notes are for rehearsal only

This arrangement © Copyright 1995 Chester Music Limited

A.B. Christmas 1909

There is no rose

15th century

John Joubert

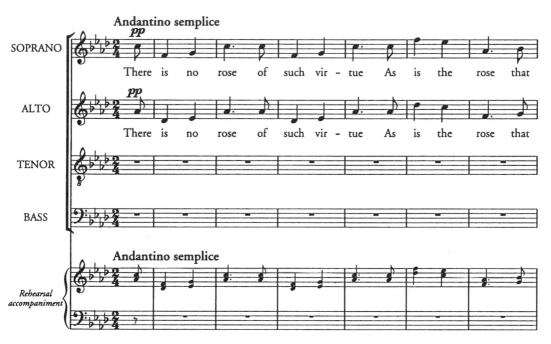

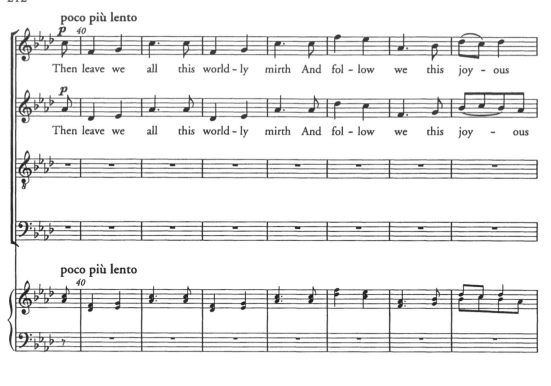

This day Christ was born

'A Carroll for Christmas day'

William Byrd
edited by Andrew Parker

For S.P.G.S.

Tomorrow shall be my dancing day

S.A.T.B. or equal/unison voices *

Traditional words

John Gardner
Op. 75 No. 2

---

* Notes on Performance

1. This piece is primarily for mixed-voice chorus. It can, however, be performed with equal voices, in which case the first three verses are sung in unison and the piano accompaniment in square brackets used. The fourth verse is apt alike for equal and mixed voice.

2. When performed with mixed-voice chorus, no accompaniment should be used for verses 1-3 unless the singers require support. All four may be performed unaccompanied, in which case verse 4 is sung to the same setting as the other three verses.

3. Percussion can be omitted, but is better included. Instruments other than tambourine and side drum may be used provided the rhythm is marked.

4. The underneath part in the descant line in verse 4 should be sung. This line can be given to women alone even in a mixed-chorus version.

call my __ true __ love __ to my __ dance: *Sing* __

call my true love __ to my __ dance: *Sing* __

O my __ love, __ O my love, my love my love, This

O my love, O my love, my love, my love, This have

The twelve days of Christmas

English traditional

arr. Andrew Carter

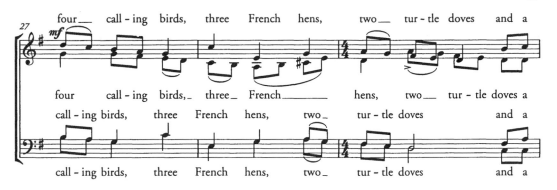

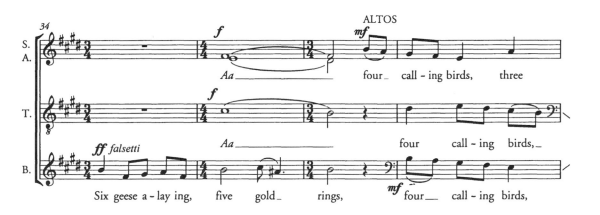

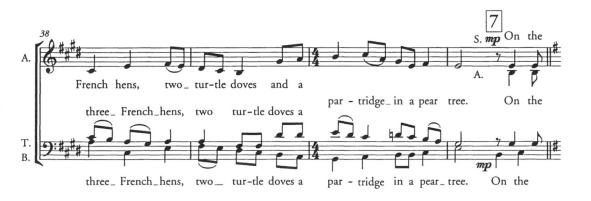

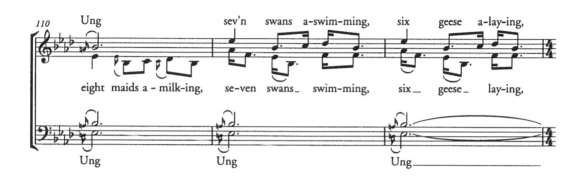

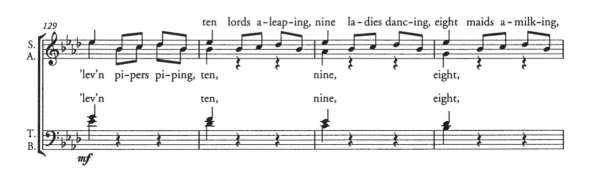

Bishopshorpe, York
December 1971
Revised 1975

We three kings

John Henry Hopkins

John Henry Hopkins
arr. Ralph Allwood

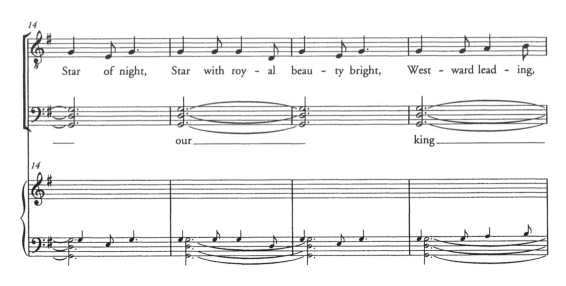

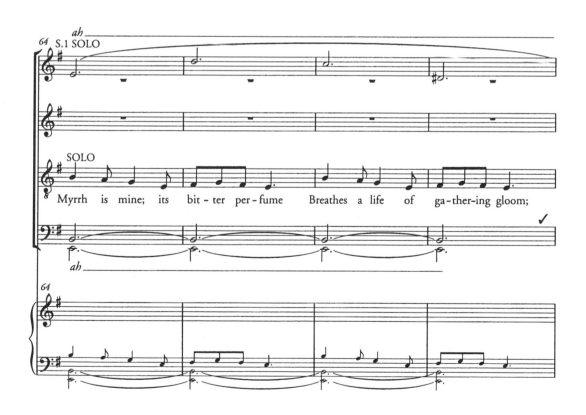

Sor-rowing, sigh - ing, bleed - ing, dy - ing, Sealed in the stone - cold tomb. O

Star of Won - der, Star of Night, Star with roy - al beau - ty bright,

ah _____ O star, _____ O

ah

We wish you a merry Christmas

trad., arr. Ralph Allwood

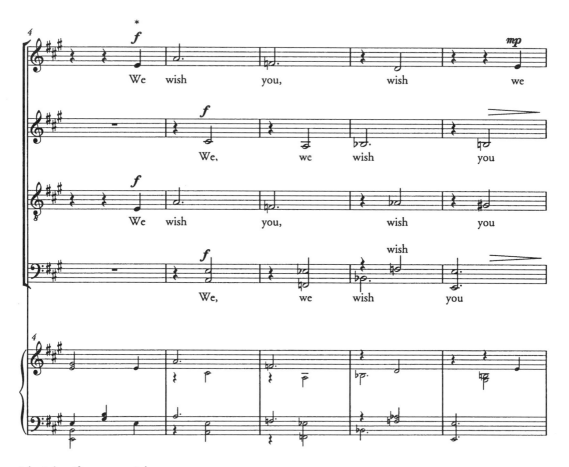

* begin here if unaccompanied

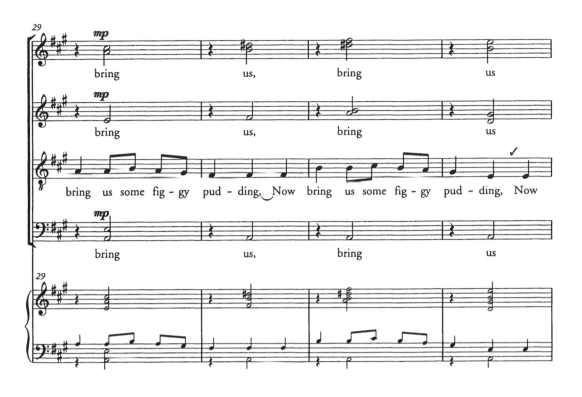

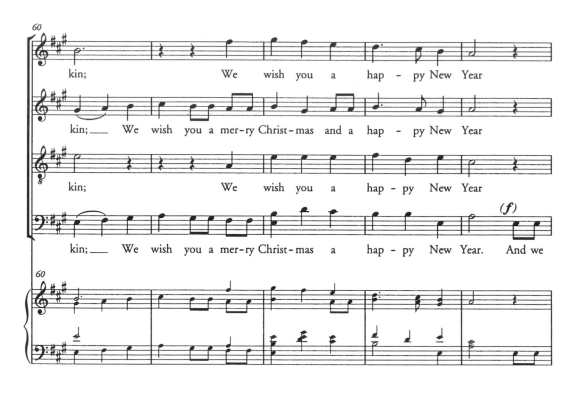

While shepherds watched their flocks by night

Nahum Tate

after Christopher Tye
verse 6 arr. Clement McWilliam

1. While shep - herds watched their flocks by night, All

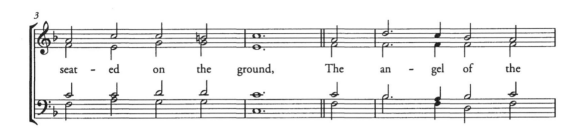

seat - ed on the ground, The an - gel of the

Lord came down, And glo - ry shone a - round.

2. 'Fear not,' said he (for mighty dread
   Had seized their troubled mind);
   'Glad tidings of great joy I bring
   To you and all mankind.

3. 'To you in David's town this day
   Is born of David's line
   A Saviour, who is Christ the Lord;
   And this shall be the sign:

4. 'The heavenly Babe you there shall find
   To human view displayed,
   All meanly wrapped in swathing bands,
   And in a manger laid.'

5. Thus spake the Seraph; and forthwith
   Appeared a shining throng
   Of Angels praising God, who thus
   Addressed their joyful song:

264

In dulci jubilo

(p. 56): translation

1 In dulci jubilo,
In sweet joy
nun singet und seid froh!
now sing and be joyful
Unsers Herzen Wonne
Our hearts' joy
leit in praesepio,
leads us to the manger
und leuchtet als die Sonne
and shines forth like the sun
matris in gremio.
in the mother's lap.
Alpha es et O!
You are Alpha and Omega!

2 O Jesu parvule,
O tiny Jesus
nach dir ist mir so weh.
I ache for you so much.
Tröst mir mein Gemüte,
Comfort my heart
o Puer optime;
o best of boys
durch alle deine Güte,
by your loving-kindness
O Princeps Gloriae,
O Prince of glory
Trahe me post te!
Draw me after you!

3 O Patris caritas!
O love of the Father
O Nati lenitas!
O gentleness of the Son
Wir wärn all' verloren
We would all be lost
per nostra crimina;
through our faults
so hat er uns erworben
so he has gained for us
coelorum gaudia;
the joys of heaven;
eia, wärn wir da!
Oh, that we might be there!

4 Ubi sunt gaudia?
Where there are joys
Nirgends mehr denn da,
Nowhere more than there
da die Engel singen
There the angels sing
nova cantica;
new songs
und die Schellen klingen
and the sweet bells ring
in Regis curia;
in the King's court;
eia, wärn wir da!
Oh, that we might be there!

Printed and bound in Great Britain by Caligraving Limited